# THE DINOSAUR SKULL

## BY
## DOUGAL DIXON

# HISTORY HUNTERS

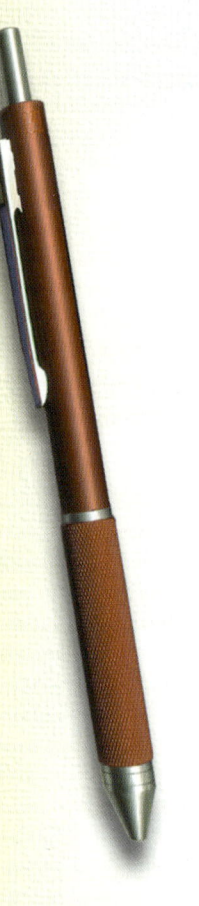

# THE DINOSAUR SKULL

ticktock MEDIA

Copyright © ticktock Entertainment Ltd 2003
First published in Great Britain in 2003 by ticktock Media Ltd.,
Unit 2, Orchard Business Centre, North Farm Road, Tunbridge Wells, Kent, TN2 3XF
We would like to thank: Dr. Angela C. Milner at The Natural History Museum and Elizabeth Wiggans.
Illustrations by Luis Rey, John Alston, Simon Mendez and Dougal Dixon.
ISBN 1 86007 370 0 PB
ISBN 1 86007 376 X HB
Printed in Egypt
A CIP catalogue record for this book is available from the British Library.
All rights reserved. No part of this publication may be reproduced, copied, stored in a retrieval system, or transmitted in any form or by any means electronic, mechanical, photocopying, recording or otherwise, without prior written permission of the copyright owner.

Would you like to join an exciting expedition to the USA?

The characters, accompanying you on the expedition, Charlie Smith, Dr. Marilyn Petronella and Professor Dean (Dino) Rockwell are fictional, but real facts about the work of museums, palaeontologists and scientists have been used to give you an accurate picture of the work they do. The dinosaur you will help to discover, Phobosaurus charlii, is also fictional, but its characteristics and the details of its life are based on facts about tyrannosaurs.

Interested to know more? Ready to dig for ancient clues?
Then welcome to the City Museum...

## CONTENTS

| | |
|---|---|
| A FANTASTIC FIND | 4 |
| A TRIP TO THE USA | 6 |
| ABOVE THE BADLANDS | 8 |
| LOOKING FOR THE SITE | 10 |
| THE SKELETON UNCOVERED | 12 |
| THE WORK STARTS | 14 |
| THE FIRST CLEAR LOOK | 16 |
| A RACE AGAINST TIME | 18 |
| IN THE LABORATORY | 20 |
| EXAMINING THE EVIDENCE | 22 |
| LIFE AND DEATH | 24 |
| A NEW TYRANNOSAUR | 26 |
| FAMOUS AT LAST! | 28 |
| GLOSSARY | 30 |
| INDEX | 32 |

**CITY MUSEUM PASS**

**Name:** Dr. Marilyn Petronella
**Department:** Head of Palaeontology
**Interests:** Dinosaurs and mammoths, digging and rock-climbing.

**CITY MUSEUM PASS**

**Name:** Charlie Smith
**Department:** Palaeontology - temporary research assistant
**Interests:** Dinosaurs and mammoths, football and computers.

TEMPORARY

# A FANTASTIC FIND

## Day 1

Well here I am spending the summer helping out in the City Museum. I'm working in the palaeontology department where they study life in the past by examining fossils. I have just made a fantastic discovery in a dusty basement storeroom - a fossilized dinosaur bone.

My boss, Dr. Marilyn Petronella, looked up the catalogue number in the museum records. It says that it is the left maxilla (the upper jawbone) of a Tyrannosaurus rex. But Dr. Petronella is not so sure. It is definitely a tyrannosaur of some kind but doesn't look quite right for a Tyrannosaurus rex. I didn't know there were different types. Apparently it's the same as having different sorts of cats like lions, tigers and cheetahs. They are all cats, but each has its own scientific name, and is slightly different. Dr. Petronella thinks that this fossil could belong to a completely new tyrannosaur.
And I found it!

CM-3500

With the maxilla is a file of old photographs and field notes from a 1920s expedition to Montana, in the USA.

### Skull of *Tyrannosaurus rex*

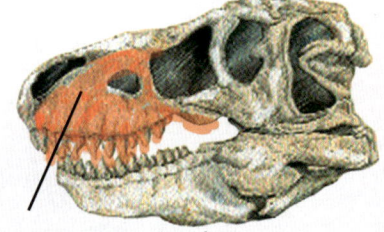

The maxilla (jaw-bone) fits in here. ← 0.75 - 1 m →

A *Tyrannosaurus rex* maxilla had about 12 teeth each about 30 cm long including the roots.

Our specimen cannot be from a T. rex. There are fewer teeth in the maxilla.

A T. rex in action in "Jurassic Park". The best movie ever!

The specimen number on the fossil means -

CM - stored in the City Museum
008 - it is specimen number 8 from the expedition.

CM-008

Palaeontologists compare newly discovered dinosaur fossils to existing ones to work out what they could be.

**Daspletosaurus torosus**
(Frightful Lizard, fleshy)
Length: 9 metres
A possible ancestor of T. rex. Smaller but with a heavy head. Had larger teeth than T. rex, but fewer of them.

The teeth on our specimen are more widely spaced.

**Nanotyrannus lancensis**
(Dwarf tyrant, from the Lance geological formation)
Length: 4 metres
The pygmy of the group. Some scientists think that it is just a baby Albertosaurus.

Our specimen much larger than this.

**Alioramus remotus**
(Different branch, remote)
Length: 6 metres
This dinosaur had a long narrow skull with horns along the crest. Lived in Asia.

Our specimen was found in the USA.

The tyrannosaurs
where does our specimen fit in?

**Albertosaurus sarcophagus**
(Lizard from Alberta, eater of the dead)
Length: 9 metres
This animal was smaller and lighter than T. rex. Possibly a fast runner.

Teeth not quite right. They are bigger on our specimen.

**Tyrannosaurus rex**
(Tyrant Lizard, king)
Length: 12 metres
This was, as far as we know, the biggest meat-eating dinosaur that ever lived.

Using the maxilla as a guide, our specimen is about 2/3 the size of T. rex.

5

# A TRIP TO THE USA

## Day 2

The 1920s expedition notes say that the maxilla fossil was found in a gully in the badlands of Montana, USA. At the end of the Cretaceous period when the tyrannosaurs lived, about 80 to 65 million years ago, Montana was a river plain by an inland sea. All kinds of dinosaur skeletons were buried in the sand and silt of the river beds. Montana today is a dry, windy place, and the land is eroding fast, exposing the fossilized dinosaurs. It is one of the best places in the world to find skeletons from the Cretaceous period.

Dr. Petronella has contacted an old friend, who is an expert on tyrannosaurs, at a dinosaur museum in Montana. He has offered to help us mount a new expedition to search for the rest of our skeleton!

Professor Dean (Dino) Rockwell with Rex the dog, in Montana.

**Montana Expedition**
Hiking boots, rucksack, water bottle, summer clothes and hat (temperatures can reach 45°C in summer), passport and US dollars.

Professor Rockwell will meet us at Missoula Airport in Montana.

Amber with an insect preserved inside. Insects become stuck in the resin from tree trunks. Over time the resin solidifies to become the mineral amber.

# Professor Dino Rockwell says "Welcome to our Museum..."

The museum was founded specifically to study the remains of dinosaurs in North America from the late Cretaceous period.

## Triceratops

These four-footed, plant-eating dinosaurs had an armoured shield around their necks, and horns to defend themselves against big carnivores (meat-eaters). They migrated in herds across the more open areas of Montana.

**FAST FACT:** The *Triceratops horridus* was bigger than a rhinoceros!

*Triceratops horridus*

## Hadrosaurus

The most common dinosaurs at the end of the Cretaceous were the hadrosaurids or duckbills. They were plant-eaters living in the thick woodlands that bordered the late Cretaceous rivers of North America.

**FAST FACT:** Their most distinctive feature was a broad, flat, duck-like beak filled with hundreds of grinding teeth!

*Hadrosaurus notabilis*

## Troodon

One of the smaller meat-eaters studied here is *Troodon formosus*. It was about 2.5 m long, and lived by hunting small prey and feeding from carrion (dead animals).

**FAST FACT:** It was a very bird-like dinosaur, probably covered in feathers!

*Troodon formosus*

---

United States of America

Montana

**From:** Professor Dino Rockwell
**To:** Dr. Marilyn Petronella, The City Museum
**Subject:** Discovery at the City Museum

Dear Marilyn,

Good to hear from you. What exciting news! As you know there have only been about 20 specimens of *Tyrannosaurus rex* ever found, and most of these have been in the last 30 years. Back in the 1920s it was recognized that the tyrannosaurs were the most powerful meat-eating dinosaurs that ever lived, but the only ones we knew of were *Tyrannosaurus rex* and *Albertosaurus*. It is not really surprising that the 1920s expedition did not get the identification quite right. From what you have said, I think that we may have a completely new type of tyrannosaur here. Come and see us Marilyn, and bring your young assistant with you. We will go to see this fossil site for ourselves.

# ABOVE THE BADLANDS

## Day 7

At last, we are in Montana, or at least above it! It is our second day here, and Dino (Professor Rockwell said it was OK to call him that) has taken us up in a hot-air balloon to show us the landscape. It's amazing what you can see from up here.

We are over the prairies, and the land is as flat as a table. The rocks have been deposited layer upon layer over millions of years. You can only see the layers where the gullies (huge, natural trenches worn in the rock by running water) and ravines (narrow, steep-sided valleys) have cut through the rocky land. These gullies form the badlands, so-called because the early pioneers found it 'bad land' to cross. Dinosaur fossils are found in the gullies. Dino tells me that under the flat surface there may be millions of dinosaur skeletons. It is only where the gullies are cut into the prairie that we can find them. But how will we find the site of the 1920s expedition?

### THE FIRST TYRANNOSAURUS REX

Natural history enthusiasts will remember this year, 1905, for many years to come. The great dinosaur hunter Barnum Brown has dug up the skeleton of a completely new dinosaur in Montana. As ever, the priority was to get the skeleton to a museum as quickly as possible, and it has been sent to Henry Fairfield Osborn at the American Museum of Natural History in New York. Osborn tells us that the dinosaur is the biggest meat-eater so far discovered. It has been named *Tyrannosaurus rex*.

Montana was not always like we see it today.
In the late Cretaceous period, 75 million years
ago, the geography was quite different.

Rivers meandered across the plains bringing sand and silt down from the Rocky Mountains. It was these rivers that deposited the sand that forms the sandstone rock of present-day Montana.

The ancestral Rocky Mountains were out on the horizon here.

There were thick forests along the river banks. This is where the dinosaurs lived.

The rivers flowed into a shallow inland sea that covered much of central North America. It stretched from here all the way down to the Gulf of Mexico.

# LOOKING FOR THE SITE

## Day 9

The prairie is so huge. When I saw it from the balloon I thought that we would never pinpoint the site. Dino said we should be able to do it by using the old photograph - it has been done before!

Using Dino's mobile home as a base we have been driving to a different area every day using farm tracks, and then exploring on foot. I nearly twisted my ankle badly yesterday scrambling down a scree slope. That is why you wear hiking boots with support around the ankle. Scree is the loose rubble that has broken from a cliff and fallen downslope.

Then suddenly today we saw a pinnacle just like the one on the old photograph. Nothing seems to have changed much in the years since the photograph was taken.

*Palaeontologist Scott Madsen exposes the lost dinosaur tracks.*

### LOST DINOS FOUND

Dinosaur footprints believed lost for ever have been found – and it is all due to some old photographs. Back in 1934 paleoichnologist (that's someone who studies fossil footprints) Roland T. Bird photographed a trail of fossil footprints in the Arizona desert. They had been there for 200 million years. 52 years later scientists wanted to have another look at them, but had no idea where they were. Then in 1986 palaeontologist Scott Madsen studied Bird's photographs. The landscape featured on the photographs led him to the exact spot. The desert sand was brushed away and there were the footprints.

*The 1920s expedition notes say the fossil bone was found here amongst the rubble at the foot of the slope.*

*The fossil will have eroded out of the rocks further up the slope. This is where we will look for more remains.*

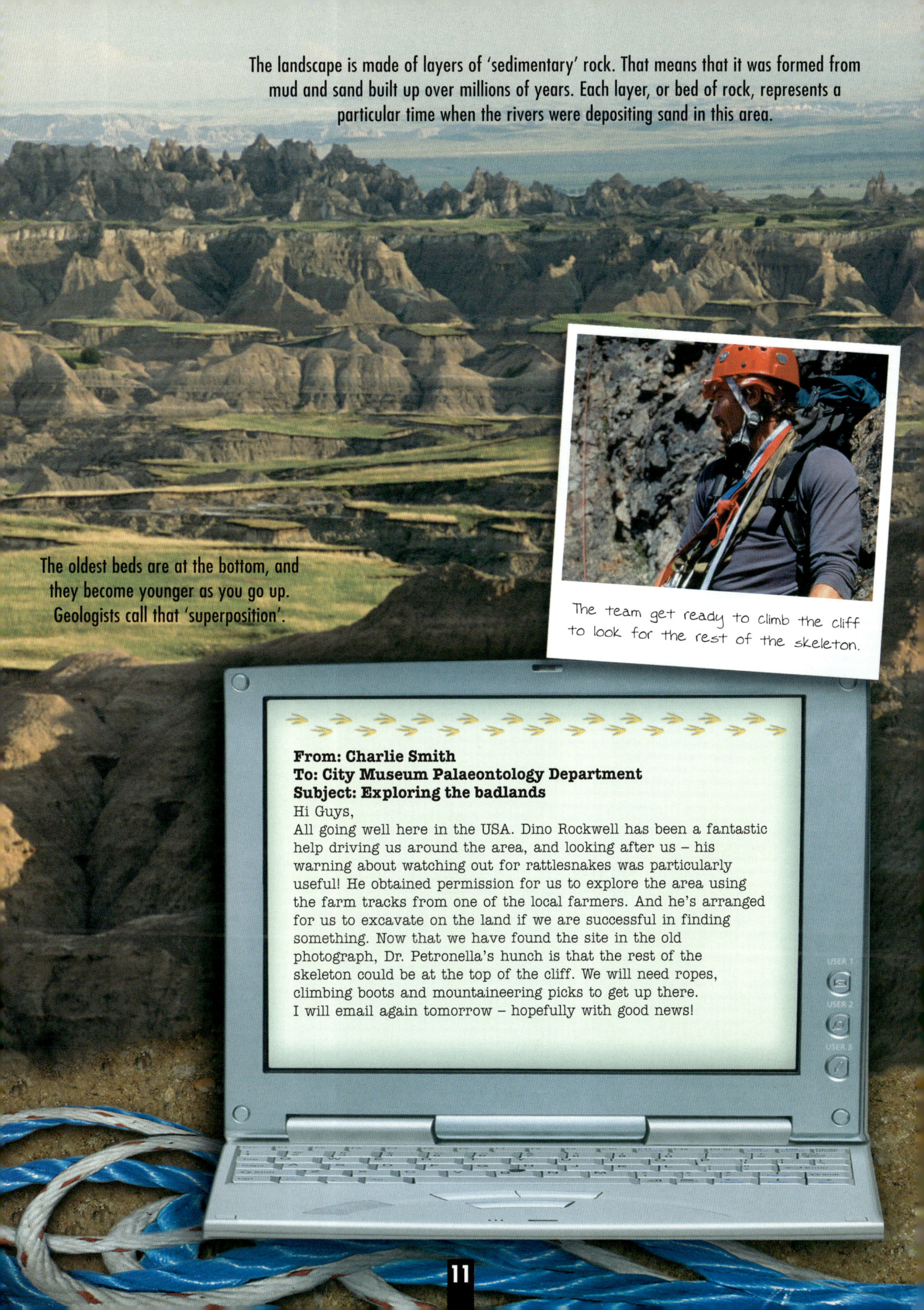

The landscape is made of layers of 'sedimentary' rock. That means that it was formed from mud and sand built up over millions of years. Each layer, or bed of rock, represents a particular time when the rivers were depositing sand in this area.

The oldest beds are at the bottom, and they become younger as you go up. Geologists call that 'superposition'.

The team get ready to climb the cliff to look for the rest of the skeleton.

**From: Charlie Smith**
**To: City Museum Palaeontology Department**
**Subject: Exploring the badlands**

Hi Guys,
All going well here in the USA. Dino Rockwell has been a fantastic help driving us around the area, and looking after us – his warning about watching out for rattlesnakes was particularly useful! He obtained permission for us to explore the area using the farm tracks from one of the local farmers. And he's arranged for us to excavate on the land if we are successful in finding something. Now that we have found the site in the old photograph, Dr. Petronella's hunch is that the rest of the skeleton could be at the top of the cliff. We will need ropes, climbing boots and mountaineering picks to get up there.
I will email again tomorrow – hopefully with good news!

# THE SKELETON UNCOVERED

## Day 10

Dr. Petronella's hunch was right! When Dino abseiled down to the ledge he found a string of fossil bones sticking out of the rock. He called them articulated cervical vertebrae. This means they are the neck bones, and that they are still joined together. Calling them neck bones is not precise enough though. Scientists must use the correct technical terms at all times so that everybody working on a skeleton knows exactly which bones they are talking about.

Dr. Petronella and I quickly climbed down, and joined Dino scraping around in the loose sandstone. Next, just a few metres away in the same fossil bed, we found a disarticulated caudal vertebrae (a piece of tail bone). Disarticulated means not joined to the rest of the tail. With the neck and tail here, is it possible that the whole skeleton is buried in the rock?

Clambering about on rock faces is dangerous. Fossil hunters wear safety helmets — in case stones fall from above — and goggles — to guard against flying rock chips.

At this exploratory stage of an excavation basic tools like hammers and chisels are used to quickly check if there are more bones deeper in the rock.

A string of articulated (joined together) cervical vertebrae (neck bones) embedded in the rock.

One of the 'Jimmy's Haulage' trucks.

**From: Charlie Smith**
**To: City Museum Palaeontology Department**
**Subject: Planning an excavation**
Hi Guys,
Dr. Petronella thinks that as the neck and tail are both here there is a good chance that the whole skeleton could be buried in the cliff! Dino wants to plan a proper excavation, but it may take as long as a year to get it all organised. We will need dozens of volunteer diggers, expensive equipment and transport – for free if possible! I can't wait to see more.

**From: The Public Relations Department, Jimmy's Haulage**
**Subject: Dinosaur transport - for free!**
Dear Dr. Rockwell,
I have just heard that your museum is planning another major dinosaur excavation. I imagine you will need a 'front loader' for lifting up the huge blocks of rock and bone, and a 'flat-bed truck' to drive them away from the site – just like on the Triceratops dig that we joined last year. We would like to offer you the use of our trucks for free if we can use this opportunity to promote our company.

# THE WORK STARTS

## One year later

I can hardly believe that it has been a year since I was here last. There has been a lot of heavy work done over the winter. Jimmy's Haulage have bulldozed a road from the nearest farm track through the badlands to the site. Now trucks and four-wheel drive vehicles can get right up to the buried dinosaur.

Soon after Dr. Petronella and I went home last season Dino's team made a small excavation on the site. It proved that there were more bones buried in the cliff. They decided to go ahead with a full-scale excavation. Hundreds of cubic metres of rock have been removed from above the specimen, and now the delicate work of excavating the skeleton begins. Dino has managed to recruit volunteers from all over the world to help as well as using the staff from his museum. And ME!

Earthmovers clear a roadway. To remove a complete skeleton a huge truck will need to get to the site.

This is the first time that the fossils have been exposed to the air for 75 million years, and they are quite delicate. Dr. Petronella is mixing up a special varnish from these white granules; this will be painted on the fossils to protect them.

The fossil bones are extremely delicate. Dental instruments and fine brushes are used at this phase of the work.

The overburden (the layer of rock on top of the fossil bearing bed) has been removed by heavy diggers.

Now we are all on our hands and knees carefully chipping away at the rock immediately above the fossil bones.

Pieces of wood that have been turned into coal show that there were trees about at the time.

The bedding pattern I've marked on the photograph shows where sand has been deposited by river currents.

This is the skull of a crocodile that we found. It must have lived in the river where our dinosaur was buried.

Important microscopic things like insect fossils and pollen grains are found in the rock and scree. We will take plenty back to the laboratory.

15

# THE FIRST CLEAR LOOK

## The best day yet!

We have removed the overburden and now we can see that we have about 40% of the whole skeleton. This is very rare. Most palaeontologists are happy if they can find a single identifiable bone. The first thing we need to do is map out all the bones as they lie. This will tell us a lot about how the animal lived and died. They are calling the skeleton Marilyn, after Dr. Petronella. They often name a skeleton after the person who discovered it. There have been T. rex skeletons called Stan, Sue and Kathy. It would have been great if it could be called Charlie, but they think its a female!

Then this evening we made the best find yet. At the foot of the cliff, in a block of scree, we found a huge section of skull. It must have broken away from the ledge. We were not looking for the skull because nobody expected it to have survived!

Almost the whole of the right hand side of the skull is here. The right maxilla looks identical to our left maxilla, and it matches up with the lower jaw from the main site.

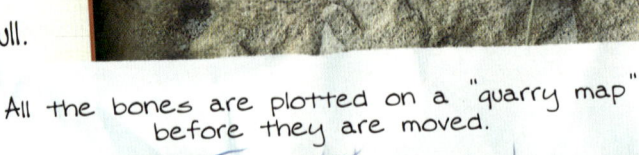

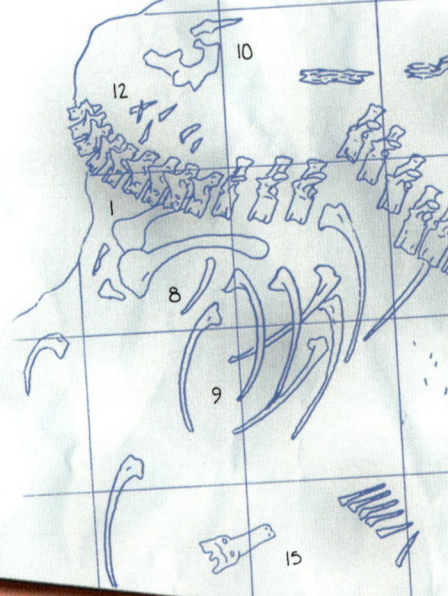

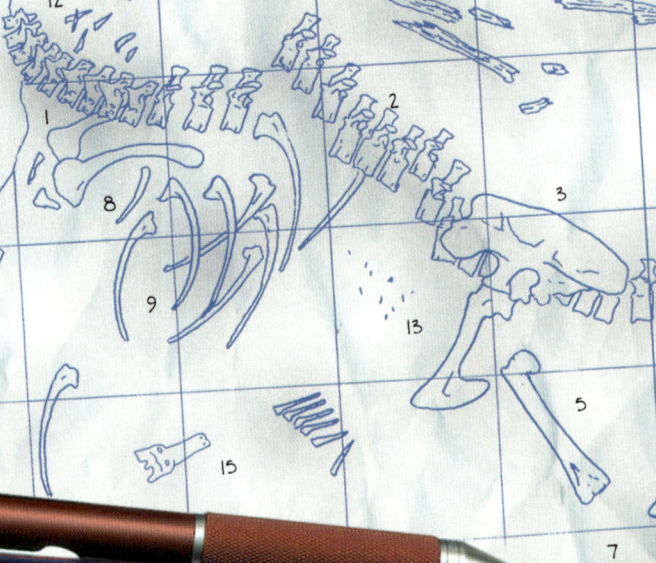

All the bones are plotted on a "quarry map" before they are moved.

As the shape of the skeleton slowly emerges from the overburden of rock a detailed diagram of what can be seen on the surface is drawn.

Digging up dinosaurs is not easy. The experts and volunteers need to work carefully and be very patient. It's easy to make a mistake, and damage a fossil.

## QUARRY MAP KEY
1. Cervical vertebrae - complete & articulated
2. Dorsal vertebrae - complete & disarticulated
3. Pelvis - almost complete
4. Caudal vertebrae - incomplete and scattered. About 40% present.
5. Right femur
6. Right tibia
7. Right fibula
8. Shoulder girdle - complete
9. Rib cage - about 50% complete - disarticulated
10. Scattered skull elements
11. Right humerus
12. Scattered bone fragments - probably cervical ribs
13. Field of broken teeth from a small theropod (meat-eater) - possibly Troodon
14. Coalified wood
15. Crocodile skull

# A RACE AGAINST TIME

## The final day

Now that we have recorded all the information we need, the time has come to take the skeleton back to the museum.

If we try to take the bones from the rock as they are they will crumble and flake away. So we cover them in plaster, just like doctors do when you break your leg. Dino says this technique was first used by a team of palaeontologists in 1876. They didn't like rice pudding, and as there was plenty of it in their expedition's kitchen they used that! Dino will cut the skeleton into manageable pieces, and we will dig a trench around each part. We have to take big chunks of the surrounding rock too, these act like splints. The problem is the season is coming to an end. If we are not careful the rains will wash everything away!

The exposed bone and surrounding rock is covered with damp paper towels. Then sackcloth soaked in plaster is spread thickly over the fossil.

We cut away at the rock beneath the fossil. Once it is freed we turn the fossil over, and plaster the other side.

**From: Lorenzo Raoul, University of eastern Patagonia**
**To: Dr. Dino Rockwell**
**Subject: reply to your email: HELP REQUIRED TO DEAL WITH FLOODING**

Dino – Sorry to hear that you have run into bad weather. This is what we did when we were almost washed out of our *Giganotosaurus* dig in Argentina last year. We cut a deep horseshoe-shaped trench in the hill around the whole specimen. The water coming downhill flowed into the trench and around the skeleton. At the same time we covered it with tarpaulins, tightly pegged down, to keep the rain off the plaster jackets. Hope this helps. Good luck!

**From: Charlie Smith**
**To: City Museum Palaeontology Department**
**Subject: Marilyn stalks the badlands again!**

Success – we have beaten the floods and the storm. Luckily the temporary roads were not washed away, and the heavy lifting gear from Jimmy's Haulage was able to get to the site. The huge blocks of plaster were reinforced by steel bars, and the skeleton was lifted piece by piece onto the truck. Once again, Marilyn is on the move across the badlands of Montana!

# IN THE LABORATORY

## Two weeks later

Marilyn is finally in the laboratory at the museum. Dino says our timing was perfect, if she had been left in the ground erosion would have destroyed her within a few years. Before the palaeontologists can study the specimen in detail the fossils must be carefully removed from the matrix (that is what we call the stone that they are embedded in). The fossils must also be preserved so that they do not decay. The specialist technicians who do this work are called preparators. They have been looking forward to this for a long time.

Before the jacketed blocks were moved from the site each one was marked with an index number. This was then keyed in to the quarry map. We took notes of what glues and hardeners were used on the fossil at the site. The preparators need to know what work has already been done on the skeleton before they start to treat it.

**VISIT OUR MUSEUM AND SEE MARILYN THE TYRANNOSAUR EMERGE FROM HER STONE TOMB AFTER 75 MILLION YEARS**

## Come watch our preparators at work as Marilyn is prepared for our paleontologists to study.

Our laboratory has a viewing gallery. Watch the team:

- Unpack Marilyn from her plaster jackets.
- Remove the embedding rock from around her bones.
- Treat the fossil bones with preservative to toughen them.
- Clean off any oxidized material from the surface of the bones and protect them from the air.
- Glue together the bones that have been broken in transit.

Newly cleaned and prepared parts of the skeleton will be displayed in the dinosaur gallery of the museum.

When work is complete the whole skeleton will be available for scientists from all over the world to study in this museum!

This tooth will be the first thing to go on display. Teeth are made of enamel, a tougher material than bones. They preserve better, and don't need much preparation.

The preparators use tiny little drills, like the ones dentists use, and high pressure air jets to clear away the rock and soft material from the fossil.

# EXAMINING THE EVIDENCE

## Dinosaur detective!

Now that Marilyn's skeleton is cleaned and prepared the palaeontologists can study it. Dr. Petronella says that in the olden days scientists would just dig the bones out of the rock, coat them with tar or some other crude preservative and stick them together on a steel framework for people to look at. Nowadays every bit of the skeleton and the surrounding rock is studied. We can find out what the animal looked like when it was alive, and how it lived.

A local hospital has even offered us the use of a CAT scan - a special kind of X-ray machine - to help us look inside the fossils. We will scan part of Marilyn's skull, and hopefully be able to see the shape of the brain case inside. This will show us the size and weight of her brain, and might even tell us which of her senses were well developed, for example did she hunt by smell? Our other investigations have shown that she was elderly, ate hadrosaurs and what's more - SHE was a HE!

adult human footprint

T. rex footprint

## SCIENCE TODAY
### NO DINOSAUR STOMPING GROUND

Scientists are deep into studying the life of a new tyrannosaur, nicknamed 'Marilyn'. In charge of the operation, Professor Dino Rockwell said 'We want to find out all we can about how Marilyn lived. It would be ideal if we could find footprints – records of her actually doing something. However the river sediments in which she was buried are not the kind of rocks in which we find fossilized footprints. There has only been one tyrannosaur footprint ever discovered, in New Mexico in 1983. There was a single print in a 2.75 m block of stone; this meant the dinosaur's stride had to be a minimum of 2.75 m. A calculation was made using its height, weight and stride length which told the scientists that the tyrannosaur walked at a speed of about 11 km/h (7 mph).'

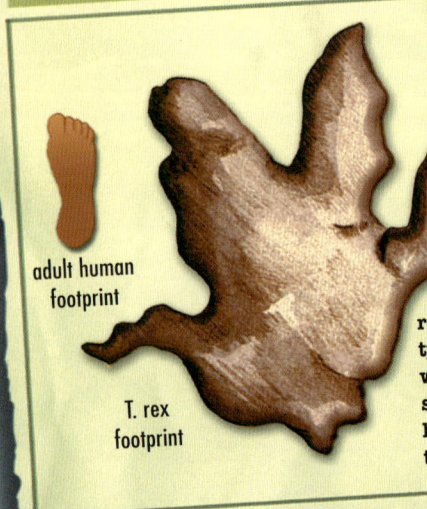

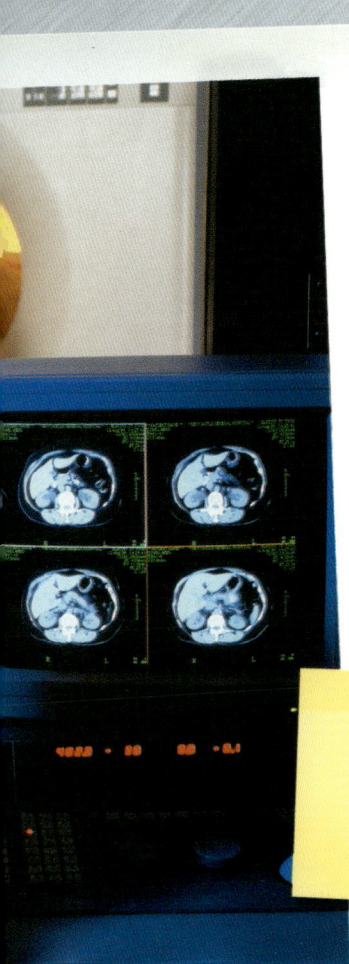

## CAT SCANS

**C**AT scanners (Computed Axial Tomography scanners) use X-rays to build up a three-dimensional (3D) image of the insides of things. They can take pictures of cross-sections (like slices) through human bodies or objects like fossils at 5mm intervals. A special computer then rearranges the slices to create 3-D pictures which can be viewed from any angle.

*Dino has told me that without a CAT scan the only way to see inside a fossil would be to smash it!*

*Microscopic analyses of the rocks have revealed pollen grains from the plants of Marilyn's landscape. She lived in mixed deciduous and coniferous woodland with an undergrowth of plants like buttercups.*

*Coprolites are fossilized droppings. They can tell us about what dinosaurs ate.*

### Investigations by Dr. Marilyn Petronella

*Coprolites from close to Marilyn are full of bits of hadrosaur bone. If the droppings are hers, she must have fed on the duckbilled dinosaurs like Hadrosaurus.*

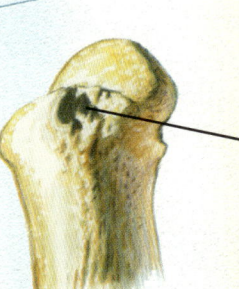

Hadrosaurus

*There is distortion at the distal joint of the tibia (the end of the leg bone furthest from the hip). Looks like gout. Marilyn must have been quite old when she died.*

*There is an extra bone called the penis retractor at the base of the tail. That means it was a male! Charlie was right after all — they should have named it after him!*

Penis retractor bone

# LIFE AND DEATH

## The whole story

Now the story is unfolding. By looking at the fossil bones, the sediments and all the other things that were buried with the dinosaur we can put the whole story together. HE lived on a river plain, and was buried in river sediment when he died. Dr. Petronella tells me that this was lucky for us. Normally when an animal dies its body is eaten up by scavenging animals. What is left just rots away - nothing to fossilize. Only when it is buried quickly is there any chance of it being fossilized. That is why dinosaur skeletons are so rare.

An information board is being prepared for display in the Museum. This will show what happened to the dinosaur after he died, but before he became a fossil - a process called taphonomy. The display will also show how the sediments became rocks, and the bones became fossils - a process called diagenesis.

1. The tyrannosaur dies, probably of old age or disease and falls into a flooded river. The floating body is caught in a tangle of jammed logs.

### 75 MILLION YEARS AGO

2. The floods die down. The body partly buried in river sediment begins to dry out in the sun. The backbone tendons shrink pulling the neck and tail upwards.

3. The meat left on the exposed part of the carcass is eaten by scavenging animals like crocodiles and small meat-eating dinosaurs like Troodon and flying pterosaurs. Bones are broken and carried away.

4. Later floods cover the remains completely with sediment. The shifting sands disarticulate the bones and move them about. Heavy animals trampling on the surface move them about too.

### 50 MILLION YEARS AGO

5. Eventually the whole site is covered by more river sediment. The geography changes, and the area sinks beneath the sea. Marine sediments build up. Sediments and bones begin to be compressed.

### 30 MILLION YEARS AGO

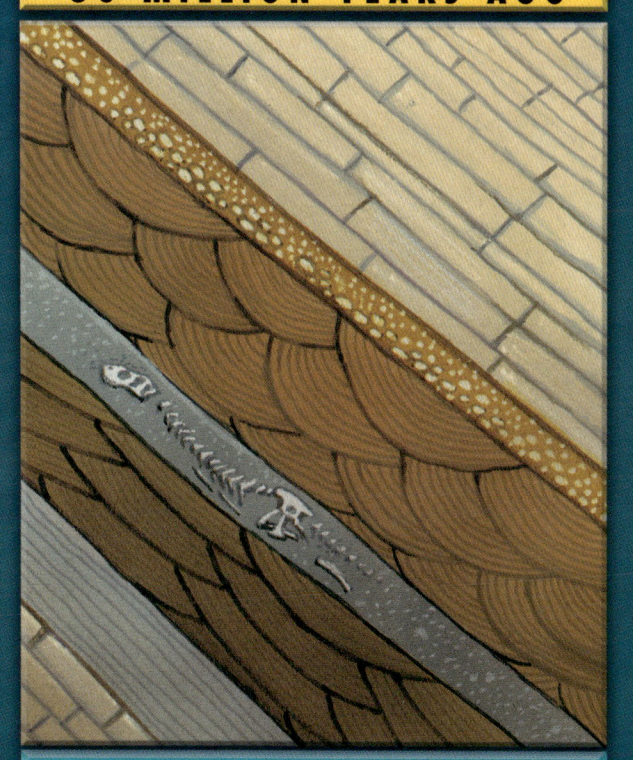

6. The sediments are crushed and cemented into rock, and the organic matter of the bones is replaced by minerals. Earth upheavals force the whole mass of rock upwards into a mountain range.

### 2 MILLION YEARS AGO

7. The weather begins to wear the rock of the mountain range away. Frost splits the stone apart. Rivers wash the rubble away. The fossil skeleton comes closer and closer to the surface.

### ONE HUNDRED YEARS AGO

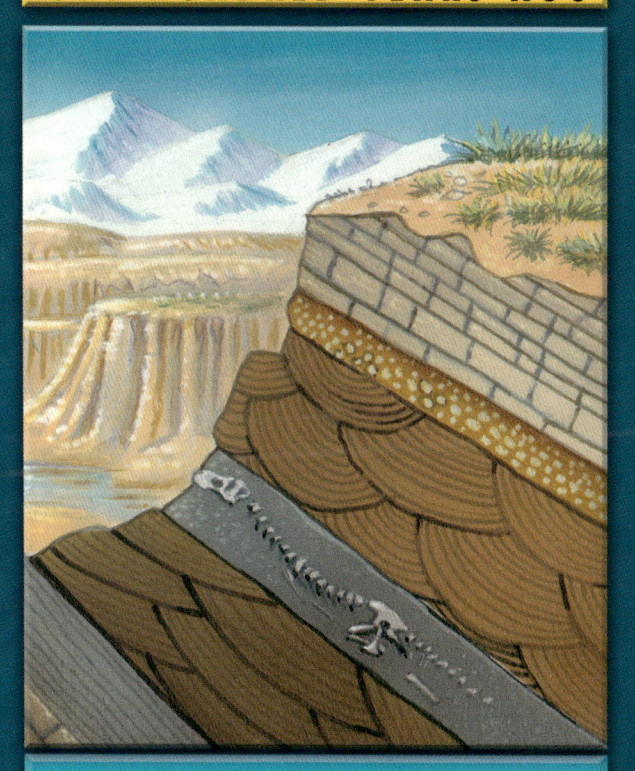

8. At last part of the skeleton is exposed – for the first time in 75 million years. It is lucky that it was spotted now. Another few thousand years and it too would have been eroded away to dust.

# A NEW TYRANNOSAUR

## A big night

At long last it is time to reveal our tyrannosaur to the world. Dino and Dr. Petronella have written up their scientific paper on everything they have found out. It will be presented today at the annual meeting of the International Association of Vertebrate Palaeontology. The paper will also be published in the Association's journal (a specialist magazine) for other scientists to read. It is all big scientific words, but that is important. Scientists from around the world who all speak different languages need to know exactly what is being described. At the same time they have put out a press release, a much simpler version of what has happened. This is sent to the newspapers and television so that they can report on the story.

Our tyrannosaur has now been given his dinosaur name too - Phobosaurus charlii. From phobos (meaning fearful in Greek), sauros (meaning lizard in Greek) and charlii - after me!

### OH REX! WHAT BIG TEETH YOU HAVE!

A new arrival to *T.rex's* family has made a big hit at a packed session of the International Association of Vertebrate Palaeontology. What the newcomer lacks in size it certainly makes up for in bite because this monster had even bigger teeth than our favourite giant meat-eater. Its upper jaw was found back in the 1920s, but lay unnoticed in the storehouse of the City Museum until it was found by a young part-time research assistant. A well preserved skeleton was dug up in Montana by the Museum's team and is currently being prepared. *Phobosaurus charlii* is named after the research assistant.

### PHOBOSAURUS CHARLII
The skull has been prepared, cleaned and mounted. It has been brought to the meeting so that scientists from around the world can see this new discovery.

# TITLE: A NEW TYRANNOSAURID FROM THE UPPER CAMPANIAN OF MONTANA

**AUTHORS ADDRESSES**  D. ROCKWELL[1] and M.P. PETRONELLA[2]
1. The Dinosaur Museum
2. The City Museum

**ABSTRACT** - A new Upper Campanian tyrannosaurid *Phobosaurus charlii*, gen. et sp. nov., is described, on the basis of a 40 per cent complete skeleton excavated from northeast Montana. The postcranial skeleton shows it to have had a conservative tyrannosaurid build but it is characterized by the relatively large teeth. Cladistic analysis places *Phobosaurus* between *Albertosaurus* and *Daspletosaurus*.

## INTRODUCTION

The serendipitous discovery of a tyrannosaur maxilla in City Museum led to the reappraisal of material gathered during the 1920s expedition to Montana. This material remained largely unpublished and the unofficial identification seemed somewhat spurious. Using photographs and field notes from the original expedition the excavation site was traced to a scree slope below an exposure of fluvial and lacustrine shales, sandstones from the Upper Campanian, similar to those search of the country rock in situ.

## SKELETAL RECONSTRUCTION

**CLADOGRAM**

Alioramus  Nanotyrannus  Albertosaurus  **Phobosaurus**  Daspletosaurus  Tyrannosaurus

## SYSTEMATIC PALAEONTOLOGY

Saurischia Seeley, 1888
Theropoda Marsh, 1881
Tyrannosauridae Osborn, 1906
*Phobosaurus charlii*, gen. et sp. nov.

**Etymology.** From phobos (Greek, meaning fearful), sauros (Greek, meaning lizard) and charlii (after Charlie, the research maxilla in the store in City Museum). erved left maxilla.

---

*Note: All scientific discoveries have to be documented properly in this way. I will have to look up all these strange new words to understand what it all means!*

# FAMOUS AT LAST!

## Opening day

It seems so long since I found that jaw bone (sorry maxilla) in the store room of the City Museum. So much has happened, and now, at last, we have built our dinosaur, and it is on display to the public. Of course, the skeleton does not consist of the original fossil bones. These are far too precious, and are kept locked away for palaeontologists from around the world to study. In the olden days a mounted skeleton like this would have been cast in plaster, but that is a bit heavy. Nowadays display skeletons are cast from lighter materials, such as glass fibre, that are easier to build with and handle. Two complete skeletons have been constructed from the casts. One has pride of place in Dino's museum, and the other is here in our own City Museum – MEET CHARLIE!

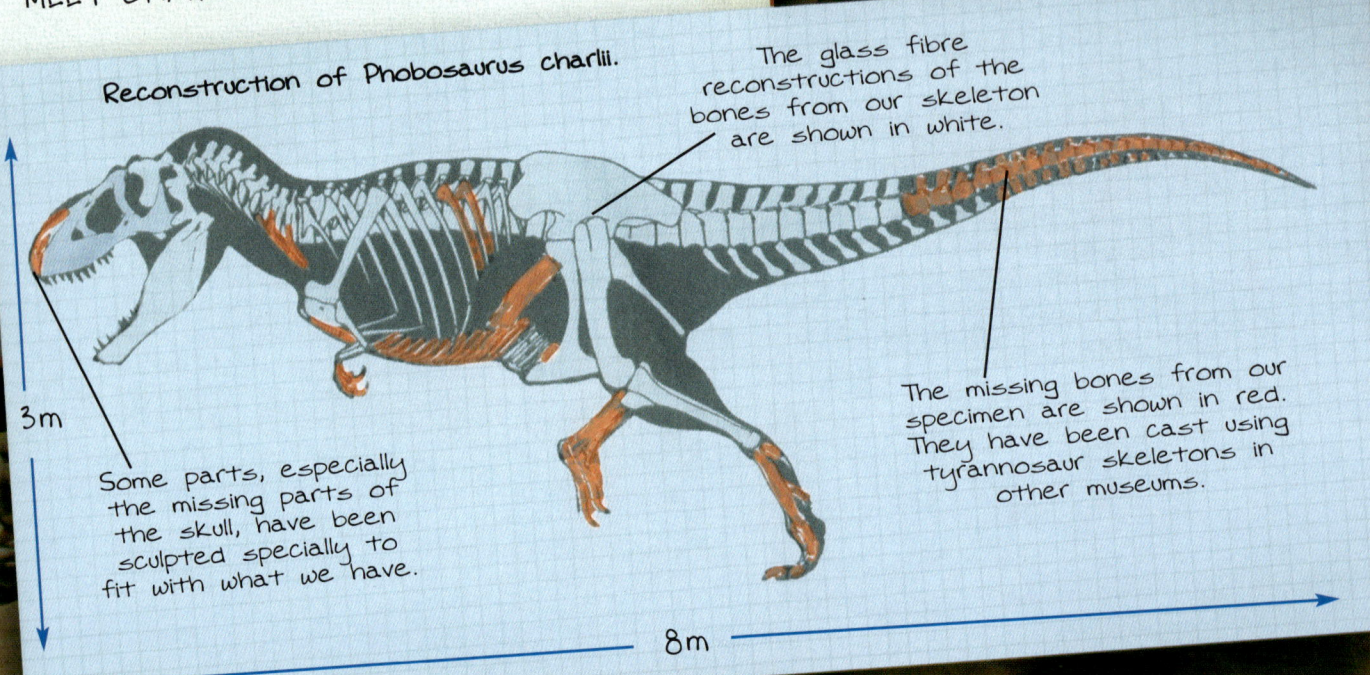

Reconstruction of Phobosaurus charlii.

The glass fibre reconstructions of the bones from our skeleton are shown in white.

The missing bones from our specimen are shown in red. They have been cast using tyrannosaur skeletons in other museums.

Some parts, especially the missing parts of the skull, have been sculpted specially to fit with what we have.

3m

8m

# MEET CHARLIE
## AT THE CITY MUSEUM

**From: Charlie Smith**
**Subject: Some worrying news?**
Dear Dr. Petronella,
I have just had a request from a research student, who is working on the classification of the tyrannosaurs, to study the *Phobosaurus* maxilla (CM-008). He suspects that it is not a new dinosaur at all, but just a new species of *Daspletosaurus*. Another researcher has just been in touch to tell me that the penis retractor bone is nothing of the sort, but that the shape of this bone is to help in egg-laying. So Charlie is a female after all! What should we do? Have we got it all wrong?

**From: Dr. Marilyn Petronella**
**Subject: Welcome to the world of science**
Dear Charlie,
Please don't worry. Scientists disagree all the time. This is what science is all about: testing ideas and trying to find out new things. The exciting thing is that we will never know everything. THERE WILL ALWAYS BE NEW THINGS TO DISCOVER!

# GLOSSARY

**Articulated** Joined together, for example the assembled bones of a complete skeleton.

**Bed (fossil)** The layer of rock in which the fossils have been buried for millions of years.

**Campanian** One of the divisions of the Cretaceous period, from 85 to 74 million years ago.

**Carnivore** An animal that eats meat.

**Coniferous** Trees that have leaves all year round. Pine trees are coniferous.

**Cretaceous** A period of geological time, from 145 to 65 million years ago. It was the last of the three periods in which dinosaurs lived. The others are the Triassic and Jurassic.

**Deposition** The process of rivers depositing (laying down) layers of sand.

**Diagenesis** The process through which sediments become rocks, and bones become fossils.

**Disarticulated** Not joined together, for example the individual bones of a skeleton that have come apart.

**Environment** All the conditions - the climate, the food supply, the landscape, the other animals and plants - in which an animal or a plant lives.

**Erosion** The process by which a rock or a landscape becomes worn away. Weather, rivers, landslides, tree roots and walking animals all cause erosion.

**Excavation** The act of digging into the ground, usually to uncover ancient remains such as fossils.

**Fossil** The remains of a once living thing - an animal or a plant - preserved in rock. Footprints can be fossilized too.

**Fossilized** When the remains of a once living thing - an animal or a plant - are preserved in rock.

**Geologist** A person who studies rocks to find out the history and structure of the earth.

**Gout** A disorder that results in crystals of uric acid compounds being deposited in the joints, causing painful inflammation.

**Gully** A ditch worn into the earth by running water.

**Herbivore** An animal that eats plants.

**Matrix** The material, usually rock, in which a fossil is embedded.

**Minerals** A naturally-formed inorganic substance with a fixed chemical composition, formed in the earth.

**Overburden** The layers of rock and soil above the bed containing the fossils.

**Oxidize** To combine with the oxygen in the air. Minerals and fossils that have been underground for a long time may be damaged by oxidation when exposed to the air.

**Palaeontologist** A person who studies animals and plants of the past. Note that this is the spelling used in Europe. The American spelling misses out the second 'a' giving paleontologist.

**Palaeontology (or Paleontology)** The study of fossils and life of the past.

**Paleoichnologist** Someone who studies fossilized footprints.

**Pollen** The particles of dust that the male part of a flower releases to fertilize the female part. Pollen grains fossilize well. They are useful for telling what kinds of plants lived at the time, and in the place where a certain rock was formed.

**Ravine** A narrow valley with very steep sides.

**Reconstruction** In palaeontology, a fossil skeleton that has been reassembled.

**Scree** Loose stones or rocky debris that piles up at the foot of a slope, or a cliff, as a result of erosion.

**Sediment** Particles of sand or mud that have accumulated at the bottom of a river, lake or the sea. The raw materials that make sedimentary rock.

**Silt** A kind of river sediment that is finer than sand, but coarser than mud.

**Specimen** A sample of something used for scientific study.

**Superposition** This is the idea that in an undisturbed sequence of sedimentary rocks, the oldest rock lies at the bottom while the youngest lies at the top.

**Taphonomy** The process that the dead body of an animal goes through - decay, disarticulation of the bones and so on - before it becomes a fossil.

The following words and terms will help to explain the scientific document on page 27:

**Abstract** The summary of a paper's contents.

**Cladogram** A diagram showing how the animal is related to others, based on how many characteristics are shared by the others.

**Etymology** What the animal's name means.

**Holotype** The specimen on which the description is based.

**Skeletal reconstruction** How the bones go into the complete skeleton of the animal.

**Systematic palaeontology** How the animal is classified - to what class (group) and family it belongs.

# INDEX

## A
*Albertosaurus sarcophagus* 5
*Alioramus remotus* 5
amber 6
American Museum of Natural History 8
articulation 12, 13, 30

## B
badlands, Montana 6, 8, 9
beds 15, 30
Bird, Roland T. 10
brain 22
Brown, Barnum 8

## C
CAT scans 22, 23
cladogram 27, 31
coal 15
coprolites 22, 23
Cretaceous period 6, 7, 9, 30
crocodiles 15, 17, 24

## D
*Daspletosaurus torosus* 5
deposition 8, 9, 11, 30
diagenesis 24, 30
disarticulation 12, 24, 30
documentation 26, 27

## E
erosion 6, 10, 20, 30
excavation 14, 30

## F
footprints 10, 22
fossilization 24, 25, 30
fossils 4, 8, 10, 24, 30
    preservation 20, 21
    protection 14, 18, 19

## G
*Giganotosaurus* 19
gout 23, 30

## H
hadrosaurs 7, 22, 23
*Hadrosaurus notabilis* 7

## I
insects 6, 15

## M
Madsen, Scott 10
matrix 20, 30
maxilla 4, 6, 16
Montana 4, 6, 7, 8, 9, 27

## N
*Nanotyrannus lancensis* 5

## O
Osborn, Henry Fairfield 8
overburden 15, 16, 17, 30

## P
palaeontology 4, 5, 27, 31
*paleoichnology* 10, 31
pollen 15, 23, 31
preparators 20, 21

## Q
quarry map 16, 17, 20

## R
reconstruction 28, 31

## S
sediments 11, 24, 25, 31
skeletal reconstruction 31
specimen numbers 5
superposition 11, 31

## T
taphonomy 24, 31
teeth 20, 21
tools 12, 14, 21
*Triceratops horridus* 7
*Troodon formosus* 7
*Tyrannosaurus rex* 4, 5, 7, 8

## W
weathering 25

t=top, b=bottom, c=centre, l=left, r=right, OFC=outside front cover, OBC=outside back cover

Airsport: 9tr. Alamy images: 3bl, 3br, 11cr, 13cr, 14tr. John Alston: 4bc, 5cr. Corbis: OFCbr, 8br, 10-11, 10tr, 12b, 15tr, 18-19, 20bl, 26-27, 28-29. Dougal Dixon: 4c, 10b, 16br. Everett Collection: 4br. Geoscience: 18bl, 18br. Masterfile: 8-9. Natural History Museum: 5t, 15bl. Simon Mendez: 5cr, 7tl, 7cl. Luis Rey: 5bl, 7cr, 23br, 24-25. Science Photo Library: 20-21t, 22tr.

Every effort has been made to trace the copyright holders, and we apologize in advance for any unintentional omissions. We would be pleased to insert the appropriate acknowledgements in any subsequent edition of this publication.